MW01181752

The Good Shepherd

New Testament Edition

Written by N.K. Oliver
Illustrated by Alycia Pace

...the sheep hear his voice: and he calleth his own sheep by name, and leadeth them out. And when he putteth forth his own sheep, he goeth before them, and the sheep follow him: for they know his voice...I am the good shepherd, and know my sheep, and am known of mine. As the Father knoweth me, even so know I the Father: and I lay down my life for the sheep.

John 10:3-4, 14-15

NEWTRADITIONCRAFTS.COM

Bee looking for me as you learn about Jesus.....
I will *bee* hiding in every picture......

Text © 2019 New Tradition Crafts, LLC

Illustrations © 2019 New Tradition Crafts, LLC

All rights reserved. No part of this book may be reproduced in any form or by any means without permission in writing from the publisher, New Tradition Crafts, LLC at info@newtraditioncrafts.com.

The 25 Days of Christ is a registered trademark of New Tradition Crafts, LLC.

Visit us at newtraditioncrafts.com

Library of Congress Cataloging-in-Publishing Data
Names: Oliver, N.K. | Pace, Alycia, illustrator.
Title: The Good Shepherd, New Testament & Book of Mormon Edition / by N.K. Oliver ; illustrated by Alycia Pace.
Description: Duvall, WA : New Tradition Crafts LLC, 2019. | Summary: Devotional stories from the life of Jesus Christ.
Identifiers: LCCN 2019908411 (print) | ISBN 9781733231701 (softcover)
LC record available at https://lccn.loc.gov/2019908411

INTRODUCTION

There are many testimonies of Jesus Christ and this book captures only the smallest part of His life and mission. We have selected 25 stories that are some of our favorites. They include a cross-section of key events, notable teachings, and people who interacted with the Savior during His mortal life and after His resurrection.

These stories and ornaments were selected to place more focus on Christ during the Christmas season. The 25 Days of Christ advent ornament sets have since become a treasured Christmas tradition in thousands of homes around the world. This book is the perfect companion to that daily advent tradition as it helps your family learn of and connect to Christ. The New Testament references come from the King James translation of the Bible. It is good to note that "The Good Shepherd" also stands on its own as a study aid at any time of the year.

Bees hold a very special place in our hearts. They remind us to stay close to Christ and Family. They also help us remember that the goal of this life is to "Bee"-come like Him. We wanted to give your kiddos another way to "Bee" connected to the story. Help them find the Bee in each picture and ask them how they can Bee like Christ in the stories.

We know that God rewards any effort to come to Him. We believe that as you try to draw Christ into your traditions and family, His spirit will testify of the truths that are found in these pages. We are so grateful for Jesus - His birth, life, and resurrection and testify of His love for each of us. We know He will bless your family as you strive to include Him in your lives.

the Walch family

THE BIRTH OF CHRIST
Scripture Reading: Luke 2:1-7

And she brought forth her firstborn son, and wrapped him in swaddling clothes,
and laid him in a manger; because there was no room for them in the inn.
Luke 2:7

———— • ————

Mary was a righteous young woman who believed in God and in the words of the prophets. One day the Lord sent the angel Gabriel to Mary and told her she was to be the mother of God's Only Begotten Son and His name would be called Jesus. Although Mary and Joseph were startled by this news, they chose to faithfully follow God. Many months later, Joseph and Mary made the journey to Bethlehem at the decree of Caesar Augustus to pay taxes. Mary was to have her baby soon and the long journey was hard for her. When they arrived in Bethlehem, they found the city busy and crowded. Every innkeeper turned them away. With no place to stay, Mary gave birth to her baby in a humble stable. She carefully swaddled the precious child and laid Him in a manger for a crib.

LET'S DISCUSS

- God could have provided any place for Mary to give birth. Why do you think he allowed Jesus to be born in a humble place?
- What kinds of things can we do to make room for Jesus?

ANNOUNCEMENT TO THE SHEPHERDS
Scripture Reading: Luke 2:8-20

And the angel said unto them, Fear not: for, behold, I bring you good tidings of great joy, which shall be to all people. For unto you is born this day in the city of David a Saviour, which is Christ the Lord.

Luke 2:10-11

O n the night that Jesus was born there were shepherds tending to their flocks of sheep. Suddenly, an angel appeared and announced the birth of Jesus. As the angel spoke to the shepherds the sky became bright and other heavenly messengers appeared, glorifying and praising God. The shepherds were afraid at first, but the angel assured them that this was a special day. They were told where they could find the newborn King. The shepherds quickly left their fields in search of Jesus. They found Mary and Joseph and the newborn babe in a manger just as the angel had said. Because the shepherds followed the instructions of the heavenly messenger, they knew for themselves that Christ, the Savior of the world, had indeed been born. As they returned to their flocks and fields, they shared the glorious message with others.

LET'S DISCUSS

- Imagine you were in the group of shepherds. How would you respond to the angel's message?
- God chose to send heavenly messengers to simple shepherds. What can we learn about God from this story?

THE THREE WISE MEN
Scripture Reading: Matthew 2:1-15

...and, lo, the star, which they saw in the east, went before them, till it came and stood over where the young child was.
Matthew 2:9

———————— • ————————

After Jesus was born, wise men in Eastern countries saw a heavenly sign in the form of a star. They recognized that the prophecy of Christ's birth was fulfilled. These wise men traveled to find the King of the Jews so that they could worship Him. They first stopped in Jerusalem and met with the wicked King Herod. Herod was troubled by the news and felt threatened by the idea of another king taking his place. The chief priests in Jerusalem directed the wise men to search in Bethlehem because Herod wanted the wise men to find Jesus for him. When they arrived, they found the young child Jesus and joyfully presented gifts of gold, frankincense, and myrrh. These righteous travelers were warned in a dream to not return to the wicked King Herod and they departed for home a different way.

LET'S DISCUSS

- You cannot give Jesus gold, frankincense, and myrrh directly, but what gifts can you give to Him?
- What does it mean to worship Jesus and how can you do it?

YOUNG JESUS IN THE TEMPLE
Scripture Reading: Luke 2:40-52

And all that heard him were astonished at his understanding and answers.
Luke 2:47

———————— • ————————

When Jesus was 12 years old, His family traveled to Jerusalem for the Passover feast. When it was time to return home, Joseph, Mary, and the rest of Jesus's family left Jerusalem. They were traveling with a large group of friends and extended family, so Joseph and Mary thought that Jesus was somewhere among the group. After the end of their first day's journey, they discovered that Jesus was not with them. They turned around and started searching for Him in Jerusalem. It took Joseph and Mary three days before they found Jesus in the temple speaking with the priests. Mary must have been very worried about her son. She gently scolded Him for causing His parents to worry. Jesus kindly reminded Mary that He needed to be doing His Heavenly Father's business.

LET'S DISCUSS

- What can you learn about Jesus by his response to his mother Mary?

- What does it mean to you to be about God's business?

BAPTISM
Scripture Reading: Matthew 3:13-17

And Jesus, when he was baptized, went up straightway out of the water: and, lo, the heavens were opened unto him, and he saw the Spirit of God descending like a dove.
Matthew 3:16

———— • ————

John the Baptist and his disciples taught and baptized many people on the banks of the Jordan River. John taught that people needed baptism to receive a remission of their sins. He also taught them to prepare for the coming of the Messiah. Jesus traveled from Nazareth to find John so that He could also be baptized. John recognized that Jesus was the Messiah that he had taught about. John tried to humbly decline performing the baptism ordinance for Jesus. Jesus taught John that it was important for all of God's children, even Himself, to keep the commandment to be baptized. Unlike any other son or daughter of God, Jesus did not need a remission of sins, because He is the only one to keep all of God's commandments perfectly. That included the commandment to be baptized. Immediately afterwards, those who witnessed Jesus' baptism saw the Spirit of God descending like a dove on Jesus and a voice from heaven testifying that, "This is my beloved Son, in whom I am well pleased."

LET'S DISCUSS

- Why did Jesus have a desire to be baptized?
- Why is it hard to keep all of God's commandments all the time?

WOMAN AT THE WELL
Scripture Reading: John 4:5-30

But whosoever drinketh of the water that I shall give him shall never thirst; but the water that I shall give him shall be in him a well of water springing up into everlasting life.
John 4:14

———— • ————

On the road from Judea to Galilee, Jesus and His disciples stopped to rest near a city in Samaria. Jesus waited at a well when a woman from the city came to draw water. Jesus spoke to the woman and asked for a drink. The woman may have been surprised that Jesus would start a conversation with her. Many Jews did not like the Samaritans and would travel the long way around Samaria to avoid it. Jesus told the woman that He was the source of living water. The woman thought that He was talking about real water that could be drawn from a well. Jesus explained that He is the source of everlasting spiritual life. Those that follow Him would be blessed with spiritual peace and happiness. He announced to the woman that He was the Son of God, the Messiah that prophets had foretold would come to redeem all men and women. The woman felt that Jesus spoke the truth and hurried to invite others in the city to come and hear Him teach.

LET'S DISCUSS

- What did Jesus mean when He said that He would give living water?

- What can we learn from Jesus about interacting with others that are different from us?

FISHERS OF MEN
Scripture Reading: Luke 5:1-11, Luke 6:13-16

And Jesus said unto Simon, Fear not; from henceforth thou shalt catch men. And when they had brought their ships to land, they forsook all, and followed him.
Luke 5:10-11

———— • ————

So many people came to listen to Jesus teach on the shores of the lake that it was difficult for the whole crowd to see and hear him. Jesus found Simon, also known as Peter, and his partners, including James and John, working on their fishing ship and asked Peter to let Him sit in the ship and teach the people on the shore. When Jesus was done teaching, He told Peter to move the ship to deeper water and put in their nets to fish. Peter told Jesus that they had been fishing all night unsuccessfully, but then followed His instructions anyway. The nets were soon filled with so many fish that they had to call for help from their partners' boat to pull the full nets into the ships. The catch was so large that both ships were filled nearly to sinking. A miracle had happened in a way that was meaningful to these humble fishermen. After hearing Jesus speak and marveling at the miraculous catch, Jesus next invited these men to follow Him—meaning, to leave behind their daily work to journey with Him as faithful disciples.

LET'S DISCUSS

- In what ways are you a fisher of men?

- What would it be like to leave your current life and devote all your time and energy to service?

TAKE UP THY BED
Scripture Reading: Mark 2:1-12

I say unto thee, Arise, and take up thy bed, and go thy way into thine house.
Mark 2:11

———— • ————

Jesus was teaching a group of people inside a house in the city of Capernaum. So many people wanted to hear Him teach that the house was full and very crowded. Outside of the house lay a man on a bed. He was disabled with a sickness called palsy, meaning that he could not move on his own. He had been carried there by four friends. They had come to see Jesus and had faith that He could heal the man. The large crowd inside of the house made it impossible to get inside through the door. The four friends found a way to carry their friend to the roof of the house. They opened a hole in the roof and gently lowered their sick friend down to meet Jesus inside. Jesus recognized their strong faith in Him and spoke to the sick man kindly and forgave him of his sins. When the scribes questioned whether it was right for Jesus to forgive sins, Jesus showed them all a miracle by healing the sick man. Jesus told him to stand up, pick up his bed, and walk home.

LET'S DISCUSS

- How can you be as faithful and loyal as the man's friends?
- What kind of effort is required from us when we ask for help from God?

SERMON ON THE MOUNT
Scripture Reading: Matthew 5:1-16 (see chapters 5-7)

Let your light so shine before men, that they may see your good works, and glorify your Father which is in heaven.
Matthew 5:16

——————— • ———————

Jesus often taught by using stories or parables that people understood because the situations were familiar to them. In the Sermon on the Mount, Jesus gave a parable about a candle on a candlestick. When the candle is lit it gives light to all the people in the house. He explained that when other people see a good example, they want to follow that example and do good things too. He explained our actions are like fruit—some are good, and some are bad. He taught that we should love our neighbors and our enemies, to walk an extra mile with someone else, and to be generous in giving and serving others. He talked about building houses on sand and on rock, and that following His commandments is the way to have a solid foundation. Jesus taught higher and holier ways to love God and love other people.

LET'S DISCUSS

- What are some things you can do to be a light to the world?
- How are the attributes that Jesus taught different than what the world might teach?

STILLING THE STORM
Scripture Reading: Matthew 8:23-27

And he saith unto them, Why are ye fearful, O ye of little faith? Then he arose, and rebuked the winds and the sea; and there was a great calm.
Matthew 8:26

———— • ————

The disciples traveled with Jesus by ship across the sea of Galilee. The trip was long, and they continued to sail through the night. Jesus fell asleep in the ship. A storm rose with strong winds that caused the sea to become rough. The disciples became worried. The waves grew larger and started to wash over the side of the ship. The disciples were scared and thought the ship was in danger of sinking. All the while, Jesus slept peacefully in the ship. The panicking disciples woke Jesus and asked Him to do something to save them. Jesus calmly rose in the ship and commanded the winds and the waves to stop. The air and the water became very still, and the disciples marveled that He had power to control the weather.

LET'S DISCUSS

- What kinds of things cause you to feel afraid, worried, or stressed?
- How can you maintain your faith when life gets stormy and difficult?

FEEDING THE 5,000
Scripture Reading: Matthew 14:13-21

And [he] took the five loaves, and the two fishes, and looking up to heaven, he blessed, and brake, and gave the loaves to his disciples, and the disciples to the multitude.
Matthew 14:19

———— • ————

M any started to hear about the marvelous miracles of Jesus and traveled to the country side to find Him teaching. One day, Jesus taught a large group late into the day. The people did not bring any food with them. The disciples wanted to send them to the villages to buy food for themselves. Jesus told His disciples to let the people stay and to bring all the food the disciples had with them. They gave Him five loaves of bread and two fishes. Jesus took the bread and fish and prayed to Heavenly Father to thank Him for the food and blessed it, then He broke the loaves and fishes into pieces and gave it to the disciples. He instructed them to take what they were given and to distribute portions to all the people in the crowd. The multitude of more than 5,000 ate until they were full, and the disciples gathered up the leftovers—enough to fill 12 baskets full.

LET'S DISCUSS

- Have you ever been asked to do a difficult task that you didn't think was possible?
- What miracles have you experienced in your life?

WALKING ON THE WATER
Scripture Reading: Matthew 14:22-33

And when the disciples saw him walking on the sea, they were troubled, saying, It is a spirit; and they cried out for fear.
Matthew 14:26

———— • ————

Jesus sent His disciples to travel ahead by ship while He went up into a mountain to pray by Himself. When it was nighttime, the disciples were still in the middle of the sea because the wind made sailing difficult. Jesus came down from the mountain and walked out on the water to meet His disciples in the ship. When the disciples saw something that looked like a man walking towards them on the water, they were frightened. Jesus called out to them. Peter asked Jesus to let him walk on the water, too. Peter stepped over the side of the ship and began walking on the sea like Jesus, but then he started to look around at the winds and the waves and he became afraid. Peter began to sink. He called to Jesus to save him. Jesus immediately grasped onto Peter and helped him back into the ship.

LET'S DISCUSS

- How would you have reacted if you were on the ship with the disciples?

- What are some things that cause you to be distracted from following Jesus?

THE PARABLE OF THE GOOD SAMARITAN
Scripture Reading: Luke 10:25-37

Thou shalt love the Lord thy God with all thy heart, and with all thy soul, and with all thy strength, and with all thy mind; and thy neighbour as thyself.
Luke 10:27

———————— • ————————

Jesus taught a parable about a Jew that was traveling on a road from Jerusalem to Jericho. The man was attacked by a group of thieves that beat him and took all of his things. The traveler lay on the road badly injured and helpless. Soon, a priest came near and saw the injured man. He passed by and did not stop to help. Not long after, a Levite also came along and seeing the helpless man, did nothing and continued on his way. Then a third man approached. This man was a Samaritan. Jews were not kind nor friendly to the Samaritans, but this Samaritan stopped to help the injured traveler and give him aid. He put him on his animal and took the poor traveler to an inn and took care of him. The Samaritan left plenty of money for the innkeeper to pay all the injured man's expenses. Jesus finished telling this story and then asked all that heard Him to be like this Samaritan.

LET'S DISCUSS
- How can you be a good neighbor like the Samaritan?
- Why do you think the Priest and the Levite passed the injured man and didn't stop to help him?

MARY AND MARTHA
Scripture Reading: Luke 10:38-42

But one thing is needful: and Mary hath chosen that good part, which shall not be taken away from her.
Luke 10:42

—— • ——

Mary and Martha were sisters who were friends and disciples of Jesus. One day, Martha hosted Jesus in her house and Mary was there also. Mary sat with Jesus to talk with Him and hear Him teach. Martha was a very good host but was very busy with all the chores and tasks that she thought needed to be done so that her guests would feel welcome and comfortable. It was a lot of work. Martha asked Jesus to send Mary to help her with the chores. Jesus lovingly taught Martha that she was busy and worrying about many things that were good, but that Mary had chosen something better. Mary was eager to learn all that she could from Jesus and would be blessed for it. Jesus taught that some choices are good, but some choices are even better.

LET'S DISCUSS

- What lesson do you think that Jesus was trying to teach Martha?
- How can you better prioritize your activities to choose the 'good part'?

PARABLE OF THE LOST SHEEP
Scripture Reading: Luke 15:3-10

What man of you, having an hundred sheep, if he lose one of them, doth not leave the ninety and nine in the wilderness, and go after that which is lost, until he find it?
Luke 15:4

———— • ————

Jesus taught several parables of people searching for valuable lost items. He taught a parable about a shepherd that had a flock of sheep that he was caring for in the wilderness. Like a good shepherd, he noticed that one of the lambs was missing. He worried about the sheep that was lost, so he left the flock of ninety-nine sheep to search all over for the one missing sheep. When at last he found the sheep, the shepherd carefully picked it up and carried it back to the rest of the flock. Jesus is also known as the Good Shepherd. He cares for each lamb in His flock. Each lamb is valuable to Him. That includes you. Sometimes He asks us to be shepherds like Him and to go searching for those that are lost and in danger, and to bring them back to His flock.

LET'S DISCUSS
- What does God think about a person who is trying to repent and make changes in his or her life?
- How can you be like the shepherd in this parable?

TEN LEPERS
Scripture Reading: Luke 17:11-19

And one of them, when he saw that he was healed, turned back, and with a loud voice glorified God, And fell down on his face at his feet, giving him thanks.
Luke 17:15-16

———— • ————

Ten lepers were forced to live outside of their city. They could not go home because of the terrible disease they had. People did not want to get near someone with leprosy because they could catch the disease and become a leper too. Jesus and His disciples were passing near when the lepers saw Him and shouted to Him to help them. Jesus said that if they had faith, they could go straight to a priest to show that they were clean and healthy. All ten of them went right away and were miraculously healed. Nine of them went joyfully on their way home. One of the lepers returned to thank Jesus for the wonderful blessing of being whole again. Jesus expressed disappointment that the others did not show gratitude. He blessed the grateful man and sent him on his way home.

LET'S DISCUSS

- Why do you think it is important to be grateful?
- How can you best show gratitude to God and those around you?

TRIUMPHAL ENTRY AND CLEANSING THE TEMPLE
Scripture Reading: Matthew 21:1-16

And the multitudes that went before, and that followed, cried, saying, Hosanna to the Son of David: Blessed is he that cometh in the name of the Lord; Hosanna in the highest.
Matthew 21:9

———— • ————

The disciples traveled with Jesus to Jerusalem for the coming Passover feast. When they got very near the city, Jesus sent two disciples to find a donkey. When they found it, Jesus rode on the donkey as the group arrived at the city gates to enter. Many people saw Him coming and they ran to the road to meet Him. Some cut down palm branches and laid them on the road. Others took off their cloaks and coats and spread them out on the road. This was a great honor for Jesus. The crowd of people were delighted and shouted praises to Him. They called Him the son of King David and the prophet from Nazareth. Jesus went to the temple and found that many people were using it as a place of business. This was not respectful of God and the sacred temple. He was angry and chased them out. Then He called the blind and sick people to come to Him in the temple so He could heal them.

LET'S DISCUSS

- What would it have been like to be there when Jesus entered the city?

- How can we show reverence for sacred places?

WIDOW'S MITE
Scripture Reading: Mark 12:41-44

Verily I say unto you, That this poor widow hath cast more in,
than all they which have cast into the treasury.
Mark 12:43

———— • ————

A poor widow came to visit the temple in Jerusalem. Jesus was also there with His disciples. They were in a part of the temple called the treasury, where people would come in and donate money for the temple. The disciples could see that some people gave large amounts of money and others gave less. Jesus watched the widow enter and give her donation. It was a very small amount of money—only two coins. Jesus praised the widow to His disciples because even though her donation was very small, it was a lot of money to her. Jesus compared the widow to the other people in the treasury and said that she had given more than anyone else. She could have kept those two small coins for herself but giving them to the temple was more important to her.

LET'S DISCUSS

- Why does Jesus say that the poor widow has given more than all the others giving money to the temple?

- Have you ever been asked to give up your time or money when you didn't have much extra to give?

THE LAST SUPPER
Scripture Reading: Luke 22:14-20, John 13:4-17

If I then, your Lord and Master, have washed your feet;
ye also ought to wash one another's feet.
John 13:14

———— • ————

On the day of the Passover, Peter and John were sent to find a room where Jesus and His twelve apostles could gather. As they ate their simple meal together, Jesus continued to teach them. He taught them a new ordinance where they would bless bread and wine and eat and drink in remembrance of Him. Jesus humbly served each one of the apostles by washing their feet. This was a chore that was done by servants for their masters and guests. When He was done, He taught them by example that they should serve each other and all people in the way that He served them. Jesus taught them that through love and service others would recognize them as disciples of Jesus. He also taught that by keeping the commandments they were showing love for Him. Jesus took the time to pray for his apostles.

LET'S DISCUSS

- What was Jesus teaching his apostles during the Last Supper?

- By washing the apostles' feet, what kind of example does Jesus set for us?

GETHSEMANE
Scripture Reading: Matthew 26:36-45

O my Father, if it be possible, let this cup pass from me: nevertheless not as I will, but as thou wilt.
Matthew 26:39

———— • ————

After Jesus and the apostles finished the Passover, they went to the mount of Olives and came to a garden place called Gethsemane. He invited Peter, James, and John to come with Him a little further into the garden. He found a place for these three apostles and asked them to wait for Him and keep watch. Jesus was very sad. He had something important that He needed to do that would be difficult—even for Him. He was brave and courageous and prayed to his Father in heaven. Jesus prayed to know if there was another way for Him to finish His mission, but told God that He was willing to do anything that His Father asked Him to do. While alone in the garden, Jesus experienced pain and agony. God sent an angel to comfort and help Him. Jesus did these things so that He could help every son and daughter of God repent of sins, be forgiven, and be healed. He did all those things for you so that He would be a perfect Judge, Friend, and Advocate for you. He did it because He loves you.

LET'S DISCUSS
- What can we learn from Jesus's prayers to the Father?
- Jesus asked His apostles to watch and pray for Him. How can we support others during difficult experiences?

BETRAYAL AND DENIAL
Matthew 26:47-75

And Peter remembered the word of Jesus, which said unto him, Before the cock crow, thou shalt deny me thrice. And he went out, and wept bitterly.
Matthew 26:75

———————— • ————————

After Jesus was done at Gethsemane, He gathered all of His apostles again. A group of people approached the disciples. They came to arrest Jesus and take Him to the elders to be judged. Judas had betrayed Jesus and took money in exchange to help wicked people capture Jesus. Jesus was led back to the city to see Caiaphas the high priest in charge of the trial. They accused Jesus of breaking their laws and said He was guilty. They spit on Him and hit Him. Peter had followed and waited outside the palace to see what would happen. While he was there several people recognized Peter and asked if he was a follower of Jesus. Each time Peter said no, denying that he knew Jesus. After being questioned a third time, Peter heard a rooster crow and he remembered that Jesus said he would deny Him three times before morning. Peter went away sad and ashamed.

LET'S DISCUSS

- What are some situations where you might be afraid to stand up for what you believe?
- How do you feel when you read how Jesus was treated?

CRUCIFIXION AND BURIAL
Scripture Reading: Luke 23:33-56

And when they were come to the place, which is called Calvary, there they crucified him . . .
then said Jesus, Father, forgive them; for they know not what they do.
Luke 23:33-34

———— • ————

The Jewish leaders could not put Jesus to death because the political leaders were the Romans. The Roman leader was Pontius Pilate. Jesus was brought to meet him. Pilate did not find that Jesus was guilty of breaking the laws, but he was pressured by the people to condemn Jesus to die. Pilate turned Jesus over to the Roman soldiers. They took His clothes and beat Him cruelly with a whip. They made Jesus carry a heavy wooden cross to a place called Calvary. There they crucified Jesus. He hung on the cross for many hours in pain while His friends and mother gathered nearby. While He was on the cross, Jesus asked Heavenly Father to forgive those that had hurt Him. When Jesus died, a righteous man named Joseph of Arimathea asked Pilate to let him take Jesus' body. He carefully wrapped it in linen and placed it into a new tomb nearby.

LET'S DISCUSS
- Why was Jesus able to speak so kindly about those who crucified Him?
- How do you imagine the disciples felt on the day when Jesus died and in the days that followed?

RESURRECTION
Scripture Reading: John 20:1-20 (see also Luke 24:36-43)

Jesus saith unto her, Woman, why weepest thou? whom seekest thou?
John 20:15

———— • ————

Jesus died on a Friday and was buried the same day. Saturday was the Sabbath day and His disciples mourned Him as they observed the Sabbath. Sunday morning came and Mary Magdalene and other women who loved Jesus rose early in the morning to return to the tomb to finish caring for Jesus's body. The women arrived at the tomb and found that the stone that had closed the entrance had been moved. An angel was there and announced that Jesus was not inside, that he had risen. Mary went and told Peter and John that someone had taken Jesus' body. Peter and John came running to see for themselves that the tomb was empty and immediately left to tell others the news. Mary stayed at the tomb and was heartbroken. She saw a man standing nearby—it was Jesus, but she did not recognize Him. Jesus called her by name and then she knew that it was Him. Mary was the first to witness that Jesus was resurrected. He had died but was alive again just like He had said!

LET'S DISCUSS

- How do you imagine the disciples felt to see Jesus alive again?
- Why was it important that Jesus's disciples were witnesses of His resurrection?

ROAD TO EMMAUS
Scripture Reading: Luke 24:13-35

And they said one to another, Did not our heart burn within us, while he talked with us by the way, and while he opened to us the scriptures?
Luke 24:32

———— • ————

Two disciples of Jesus were walking from Jerusalem to a village named Emmaus. They talked about what had happened in Jerusalem over the last several days including the trial, crucifixion and the empty tomb. As they were talking, they were joined by another traveler. It was Jesus but they did not recognize Him. Jesus asked them what troubled them, and the two disciples explained that they were sad and confused that Jesus was dead and his body was missing. He reminded them of scriptures that taught about Jesus—what He would do and how He would die and how He would live again. When the three arrived at the village, the two disciples invited Jesus to stay and eat with them. He came into the house and blessed and broke the bread like He did at Passover. Then the two disciples recognized that it was Jesus who was with them. Jesus disappeared out of their sight and the two disciples remembered the happy, peaceful feeling of the Spirit that they felt while they had walked with Him.

LET'S DISCUSS
- Jesus taught the men about Himself from the scriptures. What have you learned about the Savior from the scriptures?
- What did the men mean when they said that their heart burned within? Have you ever felt that way before?

ASCENSION TO HEAVEN
Scripture Reading: Acts 1:1-11

And when he had spoken these things, while they beheld, he was taken up; and a cloud received him out of their sight.

Acts 1:9

———— • ————

For forty days after His resurrection, Jesus appeared several times to His disciples. Sometimes He appeared to individuals, other times He showed Himself to large groups. Jesus did this so that His apostles and other disciples could be special witnesses of all the miracles that He performed, which included the miracle of resurrection. The apostles gave special testimony that they saw Him die and then live again. On the fortieth day after His resurrection, Jesus taught and gave them instructions to be bold missionaries and invite other people to come follow Him. He blessed them all. Jesus then rose into the air toward heaven and disappeared in a white cloud. Two angels came and stood near the apostles and taught them that one day, Jesus would come again to Earth just like He had ascended to heaven.

LET'S DISCUSS
- Why do you think it was important that Jesus showed himself to many disciples over 40 days after His resurrection?
- What can you do now to prepare for when Jesus comes again?